India's
Gupta
Dynasty

*W*ith special thanks to
Rochelle Kessler of the Department of Asian Art
at The Metropolitan Museum of Art, New York City,
for her generous assistance in
reading the manuscript.

CULTURES
OF THE PAST

INDIA'S GUPTA DYNASTY

KATHRYN HINDS

BENCHMARK BOOKS

MARSHALL CAVENDISH
NEW YORK

To Mom and Dad for love and support, as well as for that first typewriter; to Stasia and Paul for boosting my computer power; to Mike for getting me interested in writing nonfiction; to Jane and Dudley for baby-sitting; to Owen for understanding when I needed to work; to my editor, Joyce Stanton, with gratitude; and to Arthur for buying me coffee and carob chips, helping me with the math, and everything else

Benchmark Books
Marshall Cavendish Corporation
99 White Plains Road
Tarrytown, New York 10591-9001

© Marshall Cavendish Corporation 1996

Library of Congress Cataloging-in-Publication Data
Hinds, Kathryn, date.
   India's Gupta dynasty / Kathryn Hinds.
     p. cm. — (Cultures of the past)
   Summary: Describes how India, under a dynasty of remarkable rulers from 320 to 550 A.D., entered a golden age of prosperity, conquest, justice, scientific advance, and artistic and literary distinction.
   Includes bibliographical references and index.
   ISBN 0-7614-0071-0
   1. Gupta dynasty. 2. India—Civilization—To 1200.   [1. Gupta dynasty. 2. India—Civilization—To 1200.]   I. Title. II. Series.
DS451.H5   1996
934'.06—dc20   95-5665

Printed and bound in Italy

Book design by Carol Matsuyama
Photo research by Debbie Needleman

Front cover: A mural painting from the Ajanta caves depicting a Buddhist saint, the bodhisattva Avalokiteshvara
Back cover: Krishna battling the horse demon, Keshi

Photo Credits
Front cover: courtesy of Dinodia Picture Agency; back cover and page 55: courtesy of The Metropolitan Museum of Art, Purchase. Florence and Herbert Irving Gift, 1991; pages 6, 24 *(top and bottom),* 48, 49, 61. 64: National Museum of India, New Delhi/Bridgeman Art Library, London; pages 7, 22: SEF/Art Resource, NY; page 9: Dinodia Picture Agency/Suraj Sharma; page 11: Dinodia Picture Agency/Ravi Shekhar; pages 12, 26, 27, 39, 53, 63, 70, 71: Dinodia Picture Agency; page 16: Dinodia Picture Agency/B. P. Maiti; pages 17, 19, 30, 32, 38, 60: Borromeo/Art Resource, NY; page 21: Hutchison Library/Michael MacIntyre; page 28: Birmingham Museum; page 29: Dinodia Picture Agency/Satish Parashar; page 33: Scala/Art Resource, NY; page 34: The Metropolitan Museum of Art, Purchase. Enid A. Haupt Gift, 1979; pages 35, 46: Victoria and Albert Museum, London/Bridgeman Art Library, London; page 36: Vanni/Art Resource, NY; page 42: American Committee for South Asian Art, University of Michigan, Ann Arbor; page 44: Museum of Fine Arts, Boston. Charles Amos Cummings Bequest Fund; page 45: Giraudon/Art Resource, NY; page 51: Art Resource, NY; page 67: Brian Vikander; page 69: Dinodia Picture Agency/Nitin Jhaverj

POEM, page 20: translation by A. L. Basham

CONTENTS

CHAPTER ONE

A MIGHTY EMPIRE

Northern India had been in turmoil for a hundred years. Anarchy and lawlessness were widespread. The land was broken up into numerous small kingdoms. Many priests believed that the end of the world was drawing near.

But the world did not end—far from it. Out of the chaos a new order arose. The bringers of this order were the Guptas (GUP-tuhs), a dynasty of remarkable rulers who unified northern India. Under the Guptas, India experienced a golden age of prosperity, law and justice, scientific advance, and artistic and literary achievement.

The Guptas were enthusiastic patrons of all the arts. Plays and dance performances, such as the one being enjoyed in this fifth-century relief, were often presented at court.

The Rise of the Guptas

In a region where many small kings and tribal chiefs vied for power, one tribe, the Lichchavis (LICH-chuh-vihs), had gained

This lively palace scene, painted by a Gupta artist, reflects the vitality of life at the courts of the emperors.

prominence by the early fourth century. The Lichchavis were making the most of the lack of strong central control in northeastern India. As they had centuries earlier, they again enjoyed great importance in the ancient kingdom of Magadha (ma-GAD-huh). Their influence spread even to Nepal and Tibet.

Given the position of her tribe, the wedding of the Lichchavi princess Kumaradevi (ku-MAH-ruh-DEH-vee) must have been a great and splendid occasion—special gold coins were even minted to commemorate it. And with this marriage, Kumaradevi's new husband's rise to power was assured. His name was Chandra (CHAN-druh) Gupta.

Chandra Gupta was the son of a local king. His new connections with the warlike Lichchavis gave him the military strength he needed to expand his domain. This was the beginning of the Gupta Empire, and Chandra Gupta took the title Maharajadhiraja (MA-hah-RAH-juhd-hih-RAH-jah)—"great king over kings."

He ruled for about fifteen years. Then, in his old age, he decided not to pass his kingdom on to his eldest son, as was the general custom. Instead, he held a great royal audience and, before all the gathered courtiers, announced that another son, Samudra (sa-MU-druh) Gupta, would succeed him. Historians say that after this, Chandra Gupta apparently abdicated his throne; it is tempting to imagine that he did so at the very same royal audience, which would have made for a dramatic scene indeed.

In any case, around the year 335 C.E.* Samudra Gupta began his rule. He made his capital at Pataliputra (PAH-tuh-lih-PU-truh), which had been the capital of an earlier realm, the ancient Maurya Empire. Now it became the center of an even greater empire.

*Many systems of dating have been used by different cultures throughout history. This series of books uses B.C.E. (Before Common Era) and C.E. (Common Era) instead of B.C. (Before Christ) and A.D. (Anno Domini) out of respect for the diversity of the world's peoples.

THE HORSE SACRIFICE

Samudra Gupta revived the ancient custom of the *ashvamedha* (ASH-va-MEHD-huh), the horse sacrifice, which only great conquerors were entitled to perform. For the year before the actual sacrifice, a white stallion blessed by priests wandered at will. The rulers of the territories where it wandered tried to kill or capture it. If they did not, they were bound to accept the conqueror's authority over them. At the end of the year, the stallion was sacrificed in a great ritual. As priests chanted, the stallion's power was symbolically transferred to the chief queen, who passed it on to the king. In this way he was revitalized and strengthened so that he would be the best possible ruler. Samudra Gupta's grandson Kumara Gupta also performed the *ashvamedha*.

Samudra Gupta overthrew nine kingdoms in northern India, making them part of his own realm. He conquered more kingdoms in the eastern Deccan (the central portion of India), allowing the defeated kings to keep their thrones so long as they gave him tribute and homage. The warlike tribes of Rajasthan (RAH-juhst-hahn) in the northwest, along with several kingdoms on the fringes of his empire, also paid him homage and acknowledged him as their over-lord. He even received tribute from as far away as Sri Lanka, Indonesia, and Malaysia, although he had no authority in these lands.

Elephants were a prominent feature of the Gupta army, just as they are in this army on the march, painted during a later period of Indian history.

As a result of his wars, Samudra Gupta's power stretched across northern India. But the great conqueror was unsatisfied. In western India the powerful Shaka (SHA-kuh) kingdom had some-thing that Samudra Gupta still didn't have: access to the Arabian Sea. The thriving import-export business of the Shaka port cities made their kingdom a rich one indeed. Samudra Gupta wanted to conquer the Shakas so much that one of his inscriptions (words carved on monuments or buildings to proclaim the ruler's great deeds) even asserted—in very vague terms—that he received homage from the "Shaka lords." However, this statement was probably propaganda more than anything: If Samudra Gupta had actually overcome the Shakas, he certainly would have wanted more than homage from them.

Shaka power continued to bother the Guptas. According to one story, the Shakas even managed to disquiet the empire: They won a war against Samudra Gupta's cowardly successor, Rama Gupta. It is said that he was forced to make a dishonorable peace settlement with them. However, because the people of ancient India did not record much history, it is hard to be certain of exactly what happened. Rama Gupta seems to have reigned for a very short time and then to have been replaced by his dynamic younger brother, Chandra Gupta II.

The High Point

A legend says that for twelve years Chandra Gupta II dwelled in the forest as an ascetic. (An ascestic is a person who chooses to live in poverty for religious purification). Then, at the age of thirty-two, he took the throne of the empire. Another legend tells how he made his realm so wealthy that he passed out pearls to the poor. Even today, Chandra Gupta II continues to be celebrated in Indian folktales and songs.

Behind all the stories was a generous, just ruler and patron of the arts who brought ancient India to its highest state of culture. Indeed, during Chandra Gupta II's thirty-nine-year reign (from about 376 to 415), northern India was probably the most civilized and best governed region of the world.

Like his father, Chandra Gupta II enlarged the empire by conquest, bringing it to its largest extent. He called himself Vikram-aditya (vihk-RAM-ah-DIHT-yuh)—"Son of Valor." It was he who at last defeated the Shakas. He took over their capital of Ujjayini (UH-ja-yih-nee) and made it his own. Here he gathered together poets, artists, musicians, and scientists, who were called the jewels of his court. He gave up warfare, it seems, for the rest of his reign, and instead concentrated on the arts of peace.

The Gupta court was so splendid that its culture was imitated even in kingdoms that were not under Gupta rule. Chandra Gupta II's

Chandra Gupta II was so renowned that centuries later his reign was still being celebrated, as in this painting of him with the artists, writers, musicians, and scientists who were known as the "jewels" of his court.

This graceful, expressive mural is an example of the great artistic achievements of the Gupta era.

influence spread farther still when his daughter Prabhavati (prab-HAH-vuh-tee) married the ruler of a large kingdom in the Deccan. After her husband's early death and until her sons came of age, Prabhavati ruled the kingdom, probably under the direction of Chandra Gupta II.

A Chinese traveler, Fa-hsien (FAH-SHEHN), spent nine years in India during the reign of Chandra Gupta II and wrote of the great

THE ANCIENT INDIAN ARMY

The Gupta kings did not make their conquests alone, of course. They had huge armies, which were made up of cavalry, foot soldiers—and elephants.

Elephants were the tanks of ancient India. They marched at the head of the army, breaking the enemy's ranks and smashing defenses. They wore leather armor, and their tusks were tipped with metal spikes. They carried soldiers—also in leather armor—armed with long spears, javelins, and bows and arrows.

Veterinarians as well as doctors traveled with the ancient Indian army. So did women to cook for the troops. So did merchants and prostitutes. The king brought his harem and perhaps one or more of his sons. The high-ranking officers brought along members of their families. The army with all its followers was slow and cumbrous on the march, and when they set up camp, they formed a sizable, though temporary, city.

peace and prosperity of the empire. Its cities and towns were the greatest in India, he said. Taxation was light. The numerous people were rich and happy, and constantly strove to live righteously and do good works. Even the weather was ideal!

Fa-hsien wrote that it was possible to travel from one end of the country to the other in complete safety. Serious crime was rare, and when it did occur, the criminal was simply fined—lightly or heavily, depending on the offense. The harshest penalty was for repeated attempts at rebellion—the rebel's right hand was cut off. The death penalty was never used.

Around the year 415, Chandra Gupta II died, and his son Kumara (ku-MAH-ruh) Gupta succeeded him. Although he made no new conquests, for most of his long reign he preserved the Gupta Empire intact. He also carried on his father's tradition of good government and patronage of the arts.

Troubled Times

The Gupta Empire had been at peace for over fifty years. Then, in Kumara Gupta's old age, invaders swept into India. Chief among them were the Hunas (HOO-nuhs), or White Huns. These fierce warriors were related to the Huns who were overwhelming the Roman Empire in the West at the same time.

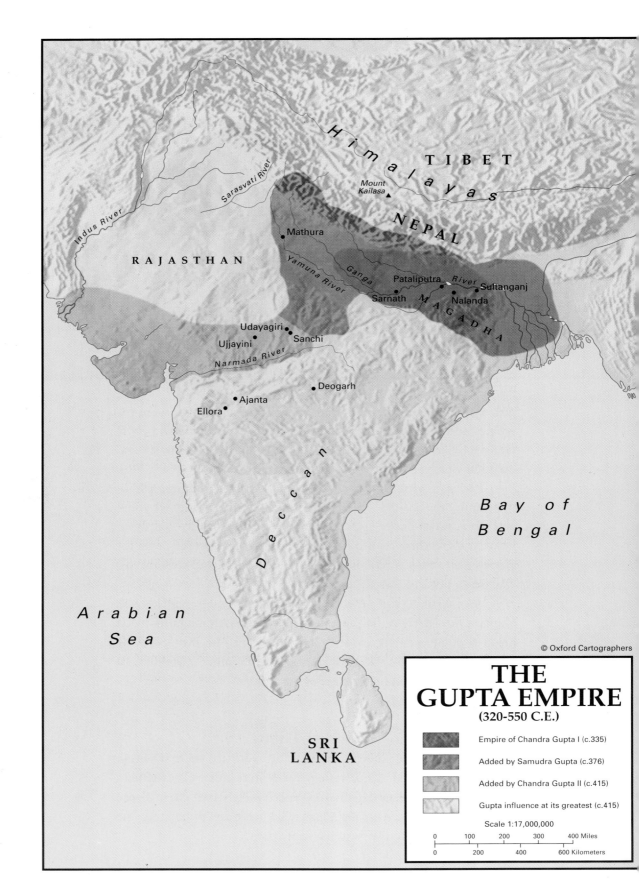

THE
GUPTA EMPIRE
(320-550 C.E.)

Empire of Chandra Gupta I (c.335)

Added by Samudra Gupta (c.376)

Added by Chandra Gupta II (c.415)

Gupta influence at its greatest (c.415)

Scale 1:17,000,000

| 0 | 100 | 200 | 300 | 400 Miles |

| 0 | 200 | 400 | 600 Kilometers |

© Oxford Cartographers

Kumara Gupta and his son Skanda Gupta went together to fight the Hunas. Just when things were at their worst, the emperor died. But Skanda Gupta carried on and at last pushed back the Hunas. An inscription of his relates how he galloped home to the palace to tell his mother of his victory.

Skanda Gupta's mother was not Kumara Gupta's chief queen, so her son was not the official heir to the throne. However, because of Skanda Gupta's great heroism against the Hunas, in 455 he became emperor anyway. He was a strong ruler, but his reign lasted for only twelve years.

The Empire Falls Apart

Skanda Gupta was succeeded by his brother Pura Gupta in 467, but within a year Pura's son Narasimha (NA-ruh-SIHM-huh) Gupta was on the throne. His reign, too, was short, as was that of his heir, Kumara Gupta II. None of these kings was able to maintain strong central control of the empire.

By the time Budha Gupta began his reign in 476—only nine years after Skanda Gupta's death—the emperor actually controlled just the eastern half of northern India. In the western half he held authority in name only. There, the descendants of provincial governors appointed by the old, strong emperors now set themselves up as hereditary kings. These kings mentioned the emperor—supposedly their overlord—only very briefly at the beginnings of their inscriptions. Then they went on to describe at length their own might. The Gupta Empire was falling apart.

In 495 the Hunas invaded again, and this time no one could turn them back. They overran western India, which remained in their power until about 533. At that time a king named Yashodharman (YA-shod-HAR-muhn) at last drove them out for good. But it was too late for the Guptas.

The Guptas had continued to lose territory. Their realm shrank to a small portion of northeastern India—an area smaller than the kingdom that Chandra Gupta had begun with two hundred years earlier. Gupta kings held on in this region for a few more decades, but by 550 the empire was completely gone.

CHAPTER TWO

A GOLDEN AGE

> "The man who knows nothing of literature, music, or art is nothing but a beast without the beast's tail and horns."
>
> —ancient Indian proverb

The unity and stability of the Gupta Empire gave people the opportunity to turn their thoughts and energies toward the arts. The Gupta kings themselves led the way: Samudra Gupta, for example, not only played the harp, but also wrote poetry that was much admired. In the empire, as well as in the territories that it influenced, literature, sculpture, architecture, and painting flowered, setting standards of achievement that would last for centuries.

Words That Moved

These artificial caves at Ajanta in the Deccan are among the most glorious monuments of India's past. Many of them were carved out during the Gupta period.

Some of the greatest works of Indian poetry and drama were produced under the Guptas. The royal courts played a major role in sponsoring literature. Poetry in particular was very much a part of court life. Poems were written to be recited at court as well as at smaller literary gatherings. Poetry competitions were often held, sometimes with the king himself participating.

The Ajanta caves are full of wall paintings that vividly portray the people of Gupta India.

The language of courtly literature was Sanskrit, which was also the language of the scriptures of Hinduism, India's major religion. Sanskrit was upper class and formal, with many grammatical rules. Educated audiences appreciated the language's complexity, and took great delight in eloquence and clever use of words.

Literature had two goals: to entertain and to stir the audience's emotions. There were eight major emotions: desire or love, mirth, anger, sadness, courage, fear, loathing, and wonder. Writers sought to present these eight in a balanced arrangement so that the audience would feel a sense of wholeness. From this wholeness arose the ninth emotion, serenity.

A poem or play therefore created a mood that allowed the audience to feel connected to great and ancient truths. In this way, literature made a link between the human and divine worlds. Basically optimistic, literature celebrated a belief in harmony among humans, nature, and the universe.

Kalidasa, the Poet

No Indian writer communicated this vision of harmony better than Kalidasa (KAH-lih-DAH-suh), one of the "jewels" of Chandra Gupta II's court. Kalidasa's poems, written in elegant, stylized Sanskrit, are full of rich descriptions and wonderful imagery. They show a great love of nature and a deep understanding of human feelings.

Only four of Kalidasa's poems have survived to the present. There are two long narrative poems, *The Birth of the War God* and *The Dynasty of Raghu,* and two shorter lyrical poems, "The Garland of the Seasons" and "The Cloud Messenger."

"The Cloud Messenger," which is just over one hundred stanzas long, has been one of the best-loved Sanskrit poems ever since it was written. It tells of a *yaksha* (YAK-shuh), a kind of minor deity, from a divine city in the Himalaya Mountains, who has been banished to central India for a year. He has had to leave his wife behind, and he misses her terribly. As the rainy season begins, he sees a cloud moving north toward the mountains, and he pours out his yearnings to it.

With beautiful descriptions of the rivers, plants, people, and cities that the cloud will pass over, the *yaksha* tells the cloud how

to reach the Himalayas. Even animals will help guide the cloud: "As you release your raindrops, the deer will show you the way." When the cloud nears the mountains, it will see the wondrous divine city with its crystal terraces that reflect the stars.

Yakshas, *like the one in this first-century carving, were earth spirits somewhat like gnomes or fairies. They served the god Kubera, lord of jewels, precious metals, and wealth.*

The poem ends with the *yaksha* describing his home and wife to the cloud. He asks the cloud to reassure his wife that he will return soon and to give her this loving message:

> *I see your body in the sinuous creeper, your gaze in*
> *the startled eyes of deer,*
> *your cheek in the moon, your hair in the plumage of*
> *peacocks,*
> *and in the tiny ripples of the river I see your sidelong*
> *glances,*
> *but alas, my dearest, nowhere do I find your whole*
> *likeness.*

Kalidasa, the Playwright

Kalidasa was not only the greatest poet of ancient India but the greatest playwright, too. While his poems were written for courtly, highly educated audiences, his plays seem to have been created to entertain a wide range of people. In fact, in one of his dramas he says, "The play, though men have many different tastes, is the one delight of all."

Kalidasa portrayed all sorts of characters. His plays included fishermen, soldiers, ascetics, jesters, courtesans, courtiers, priests, harem ladies, kings, deities, and heavenly nymphs (beautiful, divine young women). Characters fell into three classes. Women and those of the lower class spoke a common language called Prakrit. The middle class spoke a relatively simple form of Sanskrit. The highest class spoke the purest form of Sanskrit, sometimes in verse. So it seems that these plays not only had "something for everyone," but also made a conscious effort to portray society as a whole.

There were no regular theaters in ancient India. Instead, plays were staged privately in palaces or the homes of the wealthy, and publicly in temple courtyards. Costumes were elaborate, but there was no scenery and few props. Instead, props and settings were indicated by gestures. The actors, both women and men, were professionals. Sometimes, though, a king and the ladies of his harem might put on a play in the palace.

The masterpiece of classical Sanskrit drama was Kalidasa's

A LANGUAGE OF GESTURES

Acting was closely related to dancing. Both were different forms of the art of portraying the eight emotions. Both used the same intricate system of gestures. The main difference was that acting combined words with the gestures, while in dance the gestures were accompanied by music.

Princes and ladies enjoyed dancing in the palace, but most performances were given by professionals. It took years of training to learn classical Indian dance, the highest, most intricate form. All the gestures had to be mastered, as well as all the possible combinations of gestures. By Gupta times there were thirteen postures of the head, thirty-six of the eyes, nine of the neck, ten of the body, and thirty-seven of the hand.

The hand gestures, or mudras (MU-drahs), were the most notable feature of the dance—in fact, they still are; Indian classical dance is essentially the same today as it was fifteen hundred years ago. In both dancing and acting, the mudras formed a kind of beautiful code that communicated not only emotions but also character types, actions, scenery, and so on. Sculptors and painters used the mudras, too, in their portrayals of deities and the Buddha.

Classical Indian dance today uses the same elaborate code of gestures as it did in the time of the Guptas.

Shakuntala (shak-UN-tuh-luh). This play is a kind of fairy-tale romance, set in the legendary time when the human and divine worlds were not very far apart.

Shakuntala, the daughter of an *apsaras* (AP-suh-ruhs), a

The beautiful image of an apsaras *has been preserved in this fragment of an Ajanta mural.*

heavenly nymph, has been adopted by a forest hermit, Kanva. One day while out hunting, King Dushyanta (dush-YAN-tuh) arrives at the hermitage. He falls in love with Shakuntala, and she with him. They marry in an informal ceremony, but soon afterward Dushyanta is obliged to return to his capital. Before he goes, he gives Shakuntala his royal ring, promising to return for her.

Shakuntala can think of nothing but her new husband, and she neglects her duties at the hermitage. An angry hermit curses the one who is "stealing her thoughts." As a result, Dushyanta immediately forgets all about Shakuntala.

When it is discovered that Shakuntala is pregnant, Kanva sends her to be with her husband. Dushyanta does not even recognize her. She tries to show him, as proof of their marriage, the ring he gave her, only to discover that it slipped from her finger as she was bathing in the Ganga River. The king turns away, but as Shakuntala is leaving, an *apsaras* swoops down and carries her up to the sky.

Some time later, a fisherman is caught trying to sell Dushyanta's royal ring, which he found in the belly of a fish he caught in the Ganga. When the fisherman is taken before Dushyanta, the sight of the ring breaks the curse. Now the king suffers constant regret over his lost love and his harsh treatment of her.

Dushyanta is brought out of his sorrow by a summons from the god Indra, who needs the king to help fight demons. After the battle is won, Indra's charioteer drives Dushyanta through different regions of heaven. In one, he sees a little boy playing with a lion cub, and feels great tenderness toward the child. It is revealed that Dushyanta is the child's father, and now his mother enters: Shakuntala. The king falls to his knees at her feet. The family is reunited and returns to Earth to live happily ever after.

Plays with Happy Endings

Four other plays survive from the Gupta period. Two of them, both romances similar in type to *Shakuntala,* are by Kalidasa. *The Little Clay Cart* by Shudraka (SHOO-dra-kuh) is a satiric comedy, and Vishakhadatta's (vih-SHAHK-huh-da-tuh) *The Signet Ring of Rakshasa* is a political drama. Each of these last two plays has a main character who is about to be executed but is saved at the last

Images of the Buddha often communicate a great sense of peace, as in this sculpture from the fifth century.

moment. Ancient Indians did not believe in tragedy—all plays had happy endings.

Images of the Divine

Most ancient Indian art was created in the religious atmosphere of either Buddhism or Hinduism. Buddhism, founded by Siddhartha Gautama (sihd-HAHRT-huh GOW-tuh-muh), the Buddha, taught that the suffering that is a natural part of human life could be overcome by ending personal desires. In Hinduism many different deities were worshiped as expressions of the ultimate divine reality. Both religions will be described in more detail in the next chapter.

Artists worked to communicate sacred truths and inspire worshipers. Love of nature—of life itself—frequently went along with the artists' devotion to their religions. Images of animals, fish, flowers, and trees accompanied the mythological scenes

and figures carved on temple walls. The reliefs also included human beings, often women and men embracing.

Gupta sculpture was both graceful and powerful, exuberant and serene. The figures were carved according to set standards of beauty and perfection. Proportions were balanced, and distracting details were left out, so there was also a kind of simplicity. The human body was portrayed with frank naturalness.

Relatively few sculptures of the period have survived to the present, but there are many masterpieces among those that have. Two of the most notable are a seated Buddha from Sarnath and a standing Buddha from Mathura. Both of these convey the serene inner joy of Buddhist enlightenment. The image of the sun god Surya from Gwalior seems to greet his worshipers as friends. The colossal rock sculptures of the Gupta era's many cave temples and sanctuaries are moving and impressive in their power.

Besides these and other major works of sculpture, smaller pieces were produced to decorate palaces and household shrines. Sculptors also made terra-cotta (glazed or unglazed fired clay) plaques depicting scenes from literature, mythology, and everyday life. Terra-cotta figurines, some mass-produced from molds, were very common and included dolls and toys as well as religious images.

Gupta artists had a great love of nature and often portrayed plants and animals. Here a water buffalo and a horse are shown among leaves and flowers.

The sun god Surya watches over his worshipers from a magnificent height in this huge rock sculpture in the north central town of Gwalior.

THE IRON PILLAR OF DELHI

At first glance, there is nothing terribly impressive about this simple iron pillar, which was erected in honor of Chandra Gupta II. Even the ornament at the top is rather plain. But this pillar is over 23 feet (7 meters) high, and it is made of a single piece of solid iron. Further, although monsoons have rained on the pillar for more than fifteen hundred years, the iron is completely unrusted!

No one knows exactly how the iron pillar was made, but clearly it was created with great skill, care, and a huge amount of labor. To begin with, there was the feat of extracting the metal from the ore: The iron is chemically almost pure (that is why it hasn't rusted). Then there was the feat of casting such a huge and heavy piece. Nowhere else in the world was such a thing accomplished before the twentieth century. All in all, it was a remarkable achievement, and shows why the products of ancient Indian metallurgists were known and valued as far away as the Roman Empire.

Gupta artists worked in copper and bronze, too, and often on a very large scale. At the great Buddhist center of Nalanda in eastern India, there was an 80-foot (24.38 meter)-high copper image of the Buddha. In the same part of the country was found the masterpiece of Gupta metalwork, the Sultanganj (sul-TAHN-guhnj) Buddha.

Larger-than-life-size, the Sultanganj Buddha has awed viewers for nearly fifteen hundred years.

This 7 1/2-foot (2.28 meter)-high bronze statue shares the grace of the period's best sculptures in stone.

Beautiful Cities and Houses for the Gods

The towns and cities of Gupta India were spread out and airy. Houses had verandas, windows with balconies, and sometimes bathrooms. Usually they were three stories tall and were laid out in rectangles around one or more courtyards.

Everywhere were gardens, groves of trees, ponds, and even artificial lakes. On the banks of the lakes were temples and other beautiful buildings. Broad flights of steps led down to the water.

The center of the town was fortified with earthworks and a moat. In this area lived courtiers, government officials, bankers, and the like. The palace was here, too, where all the main roads met.

Palaces were built of wood and brick, lavishly decorated with gold leaf, paintings, sculptures, and silk hangings. They contained audience halls, women's quarters, and the prince's or king's private rooms, which were full of secret doors and passages. There were many courtyards, and on the palace grounds were large gardens with ponds and wooden pavilions, some built on artificial hills.

Every city had many temples. Temple architecture went hand in hand with the art of sculpture. Sculptured reliefs were used to decorate the temples, usually so lavishly that no part of a wall was left uncarved. And the temples were built in the first place to house statues of the deities.

In the time of Chandra Gupta II, Hindu temples were fairly simple square buildings and not unlike Greek and Roman temples. In fact, India had been in contact with the Greco-Roman world for centuries. During the Gupta period, many refugees from the Roman Empire's persecution of non-Christians came to India.

This painting from Ajanta gives an impression of what parts of a Gupta city were like.

This Hindu temple at Sanchi, built around 425 C.E., shows the influence of Greek and Roman architecture.

They brought with them Roman architectural and artistic ideas, which were very influential.

The new ideas were adapted and combined with native Indian ideas. By the end of the Gupta period, temples had taken on their traditional shape: a square sanctuary built in the middle of a square platform, topped by a tower or spire. The entire structure was made of stone blocks. At the four corners of the platform, or beside the steps leading up to it, were chapels for deities other than the one worshiped in the main shrine.

There were also cave temples, which were cut into cliffs and ridges. In Udayagiri (U-duh-yuh-gih-rih) in western India, twenty cave temples were carved out during Chandra Gupta II's war against the Shakas. They were filled with reliefs illustrating some of the most important episodes of Hindu mythology. Other cave temples were constructed at Ellora, in the Deccan kingdom where Chandra Gupta II's daughter was queen.

The Hindu cave temples were inspired by Buddhist cave sanctuaries, which had been around for hundreds of years. During the Gupta period, several new Buddhist caves were constructed in a curved hillside at Ajanta (uh-JAN-tah), about thirty miles from Ellora. These artificial caves have been counted among the most glorious monuments of India's past.

Some of the Ajanta caves were built as far as one hundred feet deep into the rock of the hillside. They had magnificent pillared entrances, completely surrounded by ornate carvings of Buddhist saints and symbols. A huge window over the entrance let light into a cave. Inside, at the end of a large meeting hall, was a shrine where both monks and visitors worshiped. Other caves in the complex contained living quarters for the monks.

Another kind of Buddhist sanctuary was the stupa (STOO-puh). Stupas were solid domes that contained the remains, or relics, of the Buddha or other honored individuals. Stupas were sometimes built over places where important events of the Buddha's life had occurred. Constructed of brick, the domes were often plastered or whitewashed so that they shone in the sunlight. A tower or spire frequently crowned the dome. The stupa was surrounded by a beautifully carved stone railing.

At great Buddhist centers there were many stupas, the smaller ones arranged around the main stupa. These centers also included monasteries, meeting halls, libraries, rest houses for pilgrims, and other buildings.

Paintings on the Walls

Paintings were everywhere in Gupta India. Murals decorated temples, palaces, and mansions. All cultured people were expected to be able to at least draw fairly well and to be able to give intelligent opinions about art. Yet of all this artistic activity, very little remains today.

The largest number of surviving paintings are in the Ajanta caves, where they originally covered the interior walls completely. The murals illustrate Buddhist stories, but religious scenes mix with scenes of everyday life. The whole spectrum of Gupta society

The facade of one of the Ajanta caves carved out during the Gupta period

A magnificent sense of movement is conveyed in this Ajanta painting of heavenly beings.

is portrayed, from princes and palace ladies to beggars and ascetics. There are also engaging pictures of animals, such as horses, elephants, bulls, and monkeys.

The scenes, which generally are not individually framed but blend into one another, are vivid, packed full of life and motion. Facial expressions and body movements are eloquent and graceful. Many of the images have retained their rich colors. As fine as the colors are now, they must originally have been even more brilliant. In another sense, though, the murals are as brilliant today as when they were painted—as brilliant as the era they portray.

CHAPTER THREE

TWO RELIGIONS

The Buddha founded a religion that has spread all over the world. This Gupta sculpture from Mathura in north central India is radiant with the serenity of Buddhist enlightenment.

In Gupta India two great religions, Buddhism and Hinduism, flourished side by side. Although most of the emperors were Hindus, they nevertheless made large donations to Buddhist monasteries and included Buddhists among their advisers. Fahsien, the Buddhist pilgrim from China, told of Hindu priests hosting a splendid Buddhist procession and providing Buddhist monks with their necessities. By and large, the empire was remarkable for its religious tolerance.

Buddhism

Buddhism had been in existence for over eight hundred years when Chandra Gupta came to power. Its founder was Siddhartha Gautama, who was born a prince and raised in great luxury, shielded from all the sorrows of the world. However, one day, he saw a very old man and for the first time realized that all people must grow old and weak. Soon afterward he saw a desperately sick man, and then a corpse being carried to the cremation ground followed by mourners and a wandering ascetic.

Siddhartha was greatly distressed by all of the suffering he began to see. When he met a group of five ascetics, he left with them in search of a solution to the world's sorrows. For six years he practiced meditation and fasting until he nearly died. He then realized that he was no closer to enlightenment than before. At the age of thirty-five, he seated himself under a pipal tree and vowed that he would remain there until he finally understood the causes and cures of human suffering.

For forty-nine days he meditated, even through the temptations of Mara, the spirit of worldly pleasures. Then at last he found understanding of the world's sorrows and knew how they could be overcome. He had attained Nirvana, the ideal state of perfect knowledge, understanding, and oneness with the universe. He was now the Buddha, "the enlightened one." He remained in meditation on the great truths he had discovered for another seven weeks, then set out to teach what he had learned.

The Buddha traveled from place to place, preaching sermons, founding communities of monks and nuns, and teaching people of all social classes how they might live better lives. He was honored and respected wherever he went and attracted many

The Hindu religion flowered during Gupta times and has been a major force in Indian culture ever since. Throughout its history, one of Hinduism's most beloved deities has been the god Krishna, shown in this seventeenth-century painting bringing a lotus to his beloved, Radha.

Behind the columns in this Ajanta cave, a larger-than-life-size Buddha reclines peacefully and passes into eternal bliss.

followers. After a long, peaceful ministry, he died at the age of eighty and passed into Parinirvana (PA-rih-ner-VAH-nuh), complete Nirvana—eternal bliss.

The Buddha's teaching began with the Four Noble Truths: that all existence is sorrow, that this sorrow arises from desire or craving, that the sorrow will cease when personal desire ceases, and that there is a path that can be followed to end this desire. The path is the Noble Eightfold Path, which consists of right understanding, right thought, right speech, right conduct, right livelihood, right effort, right mindfulness, and right meditation.

Right Conduct

Buddhism was (and is) a religion with a very strong code of ethics. Every day, Buddhists repeated their commitment not to injure living things, not to steal, not to "act evilly in passion," not to lie, and not to use alcohol or drugs because they tended to cloud the mind

THE BUDDHA'S THREE BODIES

It was believed that the Buddha had three bodies of different types. First was the Created Body, which was the one that lived and died on Earth. The source of the Created Body was the Body of Bliss. This was the divine Buddha, called Amitabha (a-mih-TAHB-huh), who ruled the heaven where the souls of the blessed were reborn from lotus buds. The source of the Body of Bliss was the Body of Essence, the World Soul, also called the True, the Void, and Wisdom. In fact, the Body of Essence was identical with Nirvana.

and cause carelessness. Some people also followed three additional guidelines: not to eat after midday; not to sing, dance, or take part in other amusements; and not to use perfume, jewelry, makeup, or adornments of any sort. Buddhist monks lived by all these rules and also pledged not to sleep in luxurious beds and not to accept silver and gold.

Perhaps the most influential of these moral guidelines was the first one—not to injure living things—which was also accepted by many non-Buddhists. Although the doctrine of noninjury did not stop people from fighting wars, it did promote vegetarianism. Some people went so far as to cover their mouths with a light cloth when they were outdoors so that they would not breathe in any tiny insects by mistake. In the time of Chandra Gupta II, Fa-hsien wrote, no respectable Indian ate meat or drank alcohol. Vegetarianism continues to be widely practiced in India today.

Mahayana

Roughly four hundred years after the Buddha's death, Buddhism split into two major branches. The second branch was the one that was most popular in Gupta India. It was known as Mahayana (ma-hah-YAH-nuh), "the Greater Vehicle"—greater because it offered a way to salvation for large numbers of ordinary people, whereas the older form of Buddhism was felt to be mainly for monks.

The inner core is all that remains of the sixth-century stupa at Sarnath, where the Buddha preached his first sermon. Originally the stupa had a hemispherical lower dome topped by a cylindrical upper dome, all decorated with patterned brickwork and large images of the Buddha.

Mahayana Buddhism offered people a variety of divine beings to relate to, to worship and pray to. Foremost, of course, was the Buddha himself.

By Gupta times there were many tales of the miracles performed by the Buddha. Fa-hsien recorded some of these stories as he visited the sites where they had occurred, such as the place where the Buddha let his body be eaten by a starving tiger. At another place, a monastery, Fa-hsien wrote, the monks brought out the Buddha's begging bowl every noon to make offerings. If poor people threw only a few flowers into it, the bowl would be full. Rich people, however, could not fill it to the top even with hundreds of thousands of bushels. When an invader tried to steal this miraculous bowl, he couldn't move it even with eight elephants pulling at it.

Siddhartha Gautama was thought of as the Buddha for the present age of humankind. Past ages, however, had had their own Buddhas. These former Buddhas were greatly worshiped during Gupta times; Fa-hsien wrote of stupas being built in their honor.

Also very important and popular were the bodhisattvas (BOD-hih-SAT-vuhs). These were beings who had attained

A mural from Ajanta shows the bodhisattva Avalokiteshvara holding a lotus—he was also known as Padmapani, "the lotus bearer."

enlightenment but, because of their great compassion, had decided not to enter Nirvana. Instead they remained in a state in which they could help others along the road toward enlightenment. Ultimately, all beings would become buddhas and reach Nirvana.

The most important bodhisattva was Avalokiteshvara (A-va-lo-kih-TEHSH-vuh-ruh), who was so compassionate that his helping hand reached even to the deepest purgatory, an in-between state after death, where souls were purified through suffering. Then there was Manjushri (man-JUSH-ree), who destroyed ignorance, stimulated people's understanding, and gave his worshipers wisdom and eloquence. Vajrapani (vaj-ruh-PAH-nih) was the enemy of evil. Maitreya (my-TRAY-uh), who would become the Buddha of the next age, was noted for his gentleness. Kshitigarbha (kshih-tih-GAHRB-huh) guarded the purgatories, making them as bearable as possible and doing his best to help the souls in purgatory work their way out.

Although many of the bodhisattvas were male, some were female such as Tara, a savioress and wife of bodhisattva Avalokiteshvara, and Prajnaparamita (praj-nuh-PAHR-uh-mih-tuh), who personified all the virtues of the bodhisattvas. These female deities were regarded as being more active in the world than their male counterparts.

A few centuries after the Gupta age, Buddhism all but died out in India, its birthplace. By that time, however, missionary monks had carried its teachings throughout Asia. Buddhism was well on its way to becoming a world religion.

Hinduism

The Gupta period saw the flowering of the great religion that would come to be called Hinduism (from Persian *Hindu,* "India," because it was the religion of the majority of Indians). Hinduism had no central authority or large-scale organization, yet it bound the people of India together with a set of strongly held common beliefs. Most important was the idea that each eternal soul's destiny was worked out through the interaction of karma (actions and their effects), dharma (sacred law and religious duty), and reincarnation (rebirth of the soul in a new body after death).

In Hindu philosophy, all reality was part of one vast whole. Since the whole was unknowable, and since human needs and desires were so diverse, Hindus had a large number of deities through whom they could approach the divine. Hinduism therefore embraced (and continues to embrace) a multitude of religious beliefs and practices, many of which were already very ancient in the fourth century.

In Gupta times Hindu religious devotion began to find its full expression. Devotion—usually to one particular deity—was regarded as a basic path to salvation. One way to express devotion was by *puja* (POO-jah), the ritual of worship and service to an image of the deity. The image was created with special rituals and was believed to contain the deity's life force. It would be bathed and dressed; given food, water, flowers, and jewelry; and entertained by music and dancing. In this way worshipers found a physical, human way to communicate their love for the divine essence that was so far beyond human reach.

Worshipers tended to devote themselves to one of two major deities, Vishnu (VIHSH-noo) and Shiva (SHIH-vuh). Most other deities were related in one way or another to these two.

Vishnu

Nearly all of the Gupta emperors were devotees of Vishnu. To his worshipers, Vishnu was the ultimate source of everything that is. As he slept on a thousand-headed cobra in the ocean that existed at the beginning of time, a lotus grew from his navel. From the lotus was born the god Brahma, who created the world. Vishnu then awoke and went to rule in the highest heaven.

The benevolent Vishnu was the preserver of creation. He worked constantly for the good of the world. This was why he incarnated, or took on flesh, nine times when the world was in great danger of being destroyed. His wife, Lakshmi (LAK-shmee), the goddess of good fortune, usually incarnated with him.

The best loved of all Vishnu's incarnations was Krishna (KRIHSH-nuh). Many stories of gods and heroes were combined to form the legend of Krishna.

It was predicted that Krishna, son of Devaki (DEH-vuh-kee),

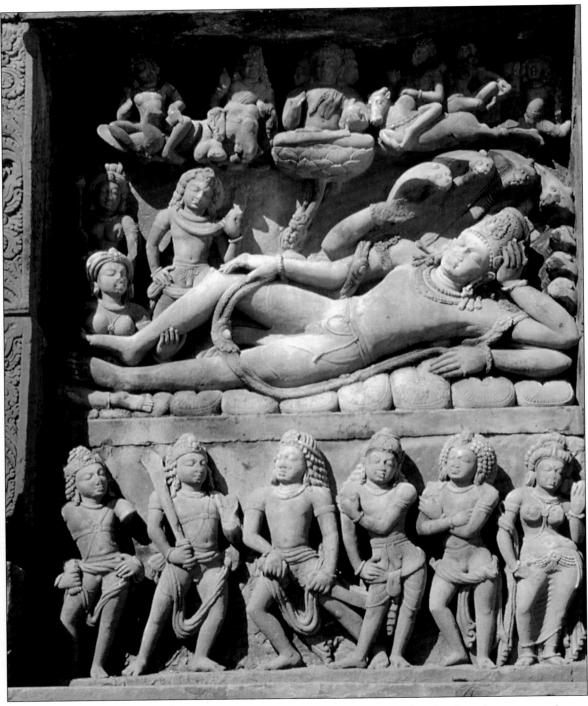

Gupta artists were famous for their fine works of sculpture. Here the Hindu god Vishnu sleeps on a cobra in the cosmic ocean.

would one day kill his cousin King Kamsa. Kamsa tried to destroy all of Devaki's children, but Krishna and his brother Balarama were saved. Thereafter, for their protection, they were raised in the country by the cowherd Nanda and his wife, Yashoda. During his childhood Krishna was delightfully naughty, playing all sorts of pranks. At the same time, he also performed many miracles and killed many demons.

The miracles and destruction of demons continued when he became a teenager. Instead of playing pranks, however, he now played the flute, and his sweet music drew the wives and daughters of the cowherds to him. He had love affairs with many of them, but especially with a girl named Radha, an incarnation of Lakshmi.

At last Kamsa found Krishna again, and the god was forced to leave the cowherds. Kamsa sent demon wrestlers to attack Krishna and Balarama, but the brothers defeated them, and Krishna slew Kamsa. Kamsa's father-in-law and another king then drove Krishna from his kingdom. Krishna founded a new capital, Dvaraka. There he had 16,000 wives, chief among them Rukmini (RUK-mih-nee), and 180,000 sons. He continued to destroy demons and evil kings all over India.

But tragedy at last befell Krishna. The chiefs of his tribe got into a drunken brawl, which spread throughout the entire city of Dvaraka. Krishna was helpless, for once, to stop the trouble. By the time it was over, Krishna's brother Balarama, his favorite son, and nearly all the chiefs were dead. In sorrow, Krishna went wandering through the forest. A hunter mistook him for a deer and shot him. The arrow pierced his heel, his one vulnerable spot. As he died, his city was swallowed by the sea.

Shiva

Shiva was (and is) a god of great contradictions. As the god of death and time, he was said to wear a necklace of skulls and to prowl battlefields and cremation grounds, with ghosts, evil spirits, and demons accompanying him. At the same time, he was the universal teacher. And as the patron of ascetics, he sat high up in the Himalayas, deep in a meditation that maintained the world.

Even as he sat meditating in mystical stillness, his divine power

THE DIVINE IN NATURE

The river goddess Ganga stands gracefully atop her sacred animal, the crocodile, in this fifth-century relief.

Deities were not worshiped in Hindu temples only; in a sense, all of nature was divine. While all of the deities had animals associated with them, some animals were sacred in their own right. The holiest animal of all was the cow. A treasure that Vishnu brought out of the cosmic ocean was Surabhi (su-RUHB-hih), the mother of all cows. The next-holiest animal was the snake, a symbol of both fertility and death. People made offerings to snakes at the beginning of every rainy season.

Plants were holy, too. Every village had a sacred tree or grove. The pipal and banyan trees were especially sacred. A tree called the *ashoka* was prayed to by women who wanted to become pregnant. Other sacred plants were a *tulsi,* a type of basil, connected with Vishnu, and *kusha* and *darbha* grasses.

All hills and mountains were holy to some extent, but the Himalayas were most holy of all. They were the foothills of the mythical Mount Meru, the center of the world, around which the deities lived.

Rivers were extremely sacred. The Ganga (or Ganges) and Yamuna (or Jumna) were personified as goddesses. It was said that the Ganga, India's holiest river, sprang from Vishnu's foot, flowed over the sky as the Milky Way, and then fell to earth through Shiva's hair. Sarasvati (SA-ruhs-VUH-tee), the goddess of literature, music, and art, was originally a sacred river.

enabled him to split his personality to become Lord of the Beasts and also Lord of the Dance. He was the inventor of 108 different dances, of all types. Never ceasing, his dancing kept the universe alive—yet one dance would destroy the world at the end of the cosmic cycle (after which the world would be created all over again).

A favorite story of Shiva was retold by Kalidasa in his long poem *The Birth of the War God.* There was a prophecy that the demon Taraka, who was terrorizing the universe, could be destroyed only by the son of Shiva and the daughter of the mountains. Since Shiva never stirred from his meditation on top of

Mount Kailasa, the other gods feared that he would never marry and father a child. Nevertheless, they asked Himalaya's beautiful daughter Parvati to go to Shiva. She, however, could not even get his attention, no matter what she tried. Kama, the love god, attempted to help her, but the flames from Shiva's mystical third eye burned Kama to ashes. (He was later restored to life.)

This fifth-century statue by a Gupta sculptor portrays Shiva with his mount, the bull Nandi.

Parvati finally decided to become an ascetic like Shiva. On a nearby mountain peak, she began her own meditations. Now at last Shiva noticed her—and fell in love with her. All the gods took part in their wedding ceremony, and in due time Parvati gave birth to Kumara, the war god. When Kumara was full-grown, he became the general of the gods and led them against Taraka, whom he slew in single combat.

Shiva and Parvati later had another son, Ganesha, who had the head of an elephant. His worship began in the Gupta period. He was a cheerful deity who loved learning and literature. He was called the Lord of Obstacles and is still prayed to by Hindus when they begin new projects or have problems to overcome.

The Goddess

Parvati was only one of many names used by the wife of Shiva. Sometimes she was called simply Devi (DEH-vee), "Goddess," or Mahadevi (MA-hah-DEH-vee), "Great Goddess." Other names were Uma (OO-muh), Kali (KAH-lee), and Durga (DER-guh). As Parvati and Uma, she was young, beautiful, sweet, and motherly. As Kali and Durga, she was fierce and fearsome, sometimes hideously ugly. In whatever form, she was (and is) the third great deity of Hinduism.

She was called Shiva's shakti, his vital energy; his power came from her. But she was an ancient deity before Shiva was ever wor-

45

This painting from the eighteenth century depicts Parvati and Shiva on top of Mount Kailasa with their children, Kumara (also called Skanda) and Ganesha. Below them, the crowd of worshipers includes Krishna (blue), *Brahma* (with many heads), *and the monkey god Hanuman.*

DEMIGODS, DEMONS, AND OTHER SPIRITS

Along with the Buddha and the great deities of Hinduism, the people of ancient India honored many other divine and semidivine beings. *Yakshas* (male) and *Yakshis* (female) were powerful spirits of prosperity and fertility who also had influence over travel, crafts, music, and dance. *Nagas* and *Naginis* were snake spirits, half human with serpents' tails. They guarded great treasures in a beautiful underground city. *Gandharvas,* who were all male, were heavenly musicians. Their female counterparts were the *apsarases,* who attended the god of love, Kama. *Apsarases* delighted in distracting ascetics from their meditations, and they sometimes raised dead heroes from battlefields and took them to heaven to be their lovers. *Vidyadharas* were heavenly magicians who could fly and change their shapes at will. They lived in mysterious magical cities in the Himalayas. *Rishis* were legendary ancient wise men who had been taken up to heaven. All of these beings were generally friendly to humans.

However, the supernatural world was also inhabited by evil spirits. The *Asuras* were the demons who were the perpetual enemies of the deities. *Rakshasas* lurked in the dark, waiting to kill and devour people. *Pishakas* haunted cremation grounds and battlefields. *Vetalas* were vampires who inhabited corpses. In addition, the spirits of those who had died violent deaths but had not received the proper funeral rites returned to their living relatives as dangerous ghosts.

shiped. She was the great mother goddess of the people of India, their protector, the giver of both birth and death.

This myth tells of her as Durga: Once again, there was a great war between the gods and the demons. The male gods could not defeat the demons and were even forced to leave the heavens. Desperate, they decided to use their own essences to create a savior. Light streamed out of all the gods. At first it looked like a flaming mountain. Then it became a beautiful young woman with her feet on the earth and her crowned head in the sky: Durga. She had one thousand arms, and the gods gave her weapons for every hand. Mounted on a lion, she then went into battle against the demons. With only a sigh, Durga produced thousands of warrior women who banged on drums and blew into conch-shell trumpets. She furiously destroyed the demons, and the gods returned to the heavens, singing her praises: "O Durga! All creatures lose their fear by praying to thee!"

CHAPTER FOUR

SACRED DUTIES

The head of a wise man, fashioned from terra-cotta in the sixth century

We have already seen the interrelationship between India's rich religious traditions and the arts that flourished under the Guptas. But religion had an even farther-reaching impact on society. In fact, nearly every aspect of daily life was thoroughly interwoven with strong religious beliefs.

Dharma

If ancient India had one central belief, it was the concept of dharma (DAR-muh). This Sanskrit word has so many layers of meaning that it is difficult to translate into English. It can mean "righteousness," "justice," "truth," "the order of things," and "sacred law." To the average Indian its most important meanings were "ethical behavior" and "sacred duty."

While all people shared the common dharma of ethical behavior, dharma in the sense of duty depended on a person's social class, stage of life, and even sex. The dharma of a woman was different from that of a man; the dharma of an elderly man was different from that of a young man; the dharma of a king was different from that of a farmer. Every person had a specific place in society, with its own particular rights and duties, and it was said that "it is better to do one's own duty badly than to do another's well."

The Four Classes

Society was divided into four great classes, called *varnas* in Sanskrit. This class system was already more than a thousand years old in Gupta times.

At the top of the social scale were the Brahmans. Brahmans were priests by class, and their primary duties were to perform religious rituals, to study, and to teach. If a Brahman could not earn his

In his sixth incarnation, Vishnu disguised himself as the dwarf Vamana in order to trick a demon who had gotten control of the world. The demon agreed to give Vamana all the land he could cover in three strides. Returning to his true, gigantic form, Vishnu strode over heaven and earth and so won them back for the deities and humans. One of the things expressed by this myth is the strong belief in divine involvement in human affairs.

living as a priest, he could hold government posts or follow certain other professions. However, he could not engage in agriculture, money lending, or selling such things as weapons, slaves, animals, or alcoholic beverages.

Next were the Kshatriyas (KSHUH-trih-yuhs)—the warriors. Kings usually belonged to this class. The Kshatriya's dharma was to protect: to fight in war and to govern in peacetime. Included in this was the duty to protect the social order and insure that all people followed their dharmas properly. A Kshatriya could also become a merchant or artisan if necessary.

The third class was that of the Vaishyas (VYSH-yuhs). Their duties were to raise cattle, to farm, and to engage in business and trade. They had fewer rights than Brahmans and Kshatriyas, but they often became quite wealthy and influential. It was among members of this class that Buddhism was most popular. Vaishyas of the Gupta Empire were noted for their charities, especially for the free hospitals they established for the poor.

On the fringes of society were members of the fourth class, the Shudras (SHOO-druhs). Their dharma was to serve the other three classes. Many Shudras, however, were free peasant farmers, and there are records of Shudra artisans and merchants. Shudras had few legal rights, and a Brahman who killed a Shudra did the same penance as if he had killed a cat or dog.

Untouchables and the Caste System

Even below the Shudras were people who were outside the class system altogether, the so-called untouchables. These included people whose jobs were particularly dirty, bloody, or menial—such as butchers, leather workers, hunters, sweepers, and those who cremated corpses—as well as people who were children of high-class women and low-class men.

The Chinese traveler Fa-hsien recorded that one such group, the *chandalas* (chan-DAH-luhs), had to live outside the boundaries of the towns and villages. When *chandalas* entered a city or marketplace, they had to strike a piece of wood to warn of their coming. If any higher-class person came into contact with a *chandala,* that person would lose his or her religious purity and would have to go through difficult and lengthy rituals to regain it.

This wall painting from one of the Ajanta caves shows courtiers and soldiers gathered around a prince.

Within the four *varnas* were many subgroups, usually known as castes—called *jati* (JAH-tih) in Sanskrit. The principles of caste were that marriage was only permitted within the caste group, food could not be received from or eaten with members of lower groups, and all members of the group were supposed to work at the same trade. In Gupta times there were many groups, such as craft guilds, that seem to have been on their way to becoming castes. But the

51

system was still forming and was not yet rigid; for example, women could marry men of higher caste (though never the other way around), and members of the same caste could find ways to work at different occupations. The caste system, which provided a measure of social security, was more important among the Vaishyas, Shudras, and untouchables than among the two most privileged classes.

Childhood

In the literature of ancient India, children were always spoken of with great affection: Kalidasa wrote that a man was blessed when children asked to sit in his lap. Parents seem to have been very tender and loving to their children and to have disciplined them quite leniently. In addition children were often pampered by the grandparents, uncles, and aunts who made up their extended family. And with all the cousins as well as siblings in the household, they always had someone to play with.

Many religious ceremonies marked the stages of children's growing up. (This again shows how important children were in Indian society.) In fact, even before birth, there was a ritual to insure the baby's well-being in the mother's womb.

When the baby was born, the birth ceremony was held before the umbilical cord was cut. Sacred chants were whispered into the baby's ear, and a mixture of honey and ghee (a kind of butter) was put into the baby's mouth. The child received a name at this time, which the parents would keep secret all during childhood. Ten days after birth, at another ceremony, the child was given a public name.

In early infancy there were rites for the baby's ear piercing and for the first time that the baby was taken outside to see the sun. Around the age of six months, the baby ate solid food for the first time, and there was a ceremony for this, too.

In a ritual when they were three years old, boys had their heads shaved. Only a topknot was left; if the boy was a Brahman and grew up to be very religious, he would never cut it. The last childhood ceremony occurred in the fourth or fifth year, in honor of the child's beginning to learn the alphabet.

Many of these rituals were probably performed only in families

In this child-naming ceremony the baby is held by a Brahman priest.

of the upper classes. In poor families children had work to do almost as soon as they could walk. Also, since daughters were not as valued as sons, some of the ceremonies may have been skipped for girls. Like Shudras and untouchables, girls were not even permitted to take part in the initiation rite that officially ended childhood.

Initiation occurred at the age of eight for Brahmans, eleven for Kshatriyas, and twelve for Vaishyas. The boy being initiated dressed as an ascetic for this ceremony. A priest gave him the sacred thread, hanging it over his left shoulder and under his right arm. The sacred thread was made of three strands of cotton (for Brahmans), hemp (for Kshatriyas), or wool (for Vaishyas). It was supposed to be left on for the rest of the initiate's life. The priest also whispered the most sacred verse of the scriptures into the boy's ear. This verse was recited at all religious rituals thereafter.

Initiation made a boy a full member of society. Although he was not yet considered an adult, he was now expected to prepare himself to follow the dharma of his class.

The Four Stages of Life

For males of the three upper classes, life after childhood was ideally divided into four stages. The first was that of student.

After initiation, a boy went to live in the home of a learned Brahman, called a guru (GUR-oo). The guru would spend hours every day teaching the Vedas (VEE-duhs), the most ancient and holy scriptures, to a small group of students, who sat around him on the ground. The students learned by rote, repeating verse after verse of the Vedas. The guru taught other subjects—such as sacred law, grammar, literature, astronomy, and mathematics—but these were of secondary importance.

Once a student had thoroughly memorized at least one Veda, he could leave the guru. However, many Brahman boys stayed to master all the scriptures, and some even pursued religious studies for the rest of their lives. Other boys did not study with gurus at all, but remained at home to learn their fathers' trades, or served apprenticeships. Buddhist boys sometimes went to study at the monasteries.

When a boy's education was complete, usually in his early twenties, he was expected to marry and begin a family as soon as possible. This was a religious duty, for marriage made him a householder—the second stage of life—and only a householder could perform the most important Hindu rituals, which took place in the home. Called the Five Great Sacrifices, these rituals were supposed to be performed every day at sunrise, noon, and sunset. They were (1) worship of the World Spirit by reciting the Vedas; (2) worship of the ancestors by pouring libations; (3) worship of the deities by pouring ghee onto the sacred fire; (4) worship of all living things by scattering grain on the threshold for spirits, birds, and animals; and (5) worship of humans by giving them hospitality.

Indians in every stage of life could relate to the legend of Krishna, which told of the god's birth, childhood, adolescence, and manhood. And at all stages Krishna was ideally heroic, as in this terra-cotta sculpture that shows him battling a horse demon.

An additional ritual was called *shraddha* (SHRAHD-huh) and was performed at every new moon by the householder, aided by Brahman priests. At the *shraddha* ceremony the householder offered special rice balls to the spirits of his father, grandfather, and great-grandfather. This insured both that the ancestors would fare well in the afterlife and that they would bless the householder and his family.

Shraddha was the ritual that truly bound the family together, and it was of the greatest importance for a man to have a son who could perform *shraddha* after he died. If his wife gave birth to no sons, and if he could afford it, a man would often take additional wives in the hope that they would bear sons. Other options were to

THE THREE AIMS OF LIFE

Householders were expected to devote themselves to the three aims of life. The first and most important of these was righteousness, and it involved following the sacred law and carrying out all of the family rituals.

The second aim of life was wealth, which should be gained honestly. It was a virtue to increase the family fortune, and wealth was also regarded as essential to leading a full life.

The third aim was pleasure, particularly the pleasure found in a man's relationship with his wife. Other pleasures were friendship, literature, theater, music, art, board games (including the game that later developed into chess), and archery contests. Amusements that were popular but not always approved of by religious authorities included gambling (usually on dice games) and animal fights, for which the most popular animals were roosters, rams, and quails.

adopt a son or to appoint a daughter to bear a son who could carry on the rite of *shraddha*.

Once a man had grandsons, he knew that his line was firmly established. Now, ideally, he should become a forest hermit, the third stage of life. He might leave his wife at home to be taken care of by their sons, or he might take her to the forest with him. He would live in a tiny hut and either eat wild plants or beg food from people in nearby villages. Most of his time would be spent in rituals at his sacred fire, study of the scriptures, and various acts of penance, such as sleeping outside in the rainy season and wearing wet clothes in winter.

If a man was truly devoted to the sacred law, in his old age he would leave even his hut and become a wandering ascetic, dressed in rags, with no belongings other than a staff and a begging bowl. Now in the fourth stage of life, he was completely detached from all worldly things. He was as ready for eternal bliss as it was possible to be.

Most men, it seems, never went past the stage of householder. Even so, if they fully performed the dharma of the householder, they were assured of a long, contented rest in heaven, followed by a happy rebirth.

Women's Lives

In Gupta India a woman's dharma was to marry, have children, and care for the home. There were exceptions: Some women became Hindu ascetics or Buddhist nuns. Some became authors of poetry and drama. Some became actors, singers, musicians, and dancers. Some even became armed guards, protecting the women of the king's household—such a guard appears as a character in Kalidasa's play *Shakuntala.*

Indian society was heavily biased in favor of males. Even before a woman became pregnant, a ritual was performed to try to insure that her child would be a boy. Parents had some practical reasons to prefer male children to females: A daughter could not perform the all-important *shraddha* ceremony. She could not carry on her father's line because she would become a part of her husband's family when she married. And usually her parents had to provide a sizable dowry or bride price in order for her to be married. But even if the birth of a female child was a disappointment, Indian parents of ancient times seem to have loved and pampered their daughters just as much as their sons.

Worshipful Wives

Although girls did not study the Vedas, well-off girls usually learned to at least read and write. They also were taught such ladylike skills as singing, dancing, painting, and making garlands of flowers. In addition to these accomplishments, courtly ladies were often described as composing songs.

A girl did not spend many years on her education; by the age of sixteen she was probably married. Her husband might be a total stranger—marriage was arranged by the parents of the bride and groom, who often met each other for the first time at the wedding ceremony. In addition, the husband might already have one or more wives, who would probably be jealous of the new bride, at least at first. All in all, many Indian girls must have found it very frightening to marry and leave the homes they had grown up in.

A wife was expected to be completely obedient to her husband and to always put his needs first. She cooked meals of rice, flat breads, and vegetables (sometimes meat) seasoned with curry, but she never ate until after her husband had eaten. She got up before him and went to sleep after him. She was expected to wait on him and to be cheerful no matter what. It was even said that a wife should worship her husband as a god—even if he had no good points at all. Divorce was never permitted.

IF YOU LIVED IN GUPTA INDIA

If you had been born during India's Golden Age under the Guptas, your way of life would have been determined by the facts of your birth—whether you were a girl or a boy; free or slave; wealthy or poor. With this chart you can trace the course your life might have taken as a member of a high class in the capital city of Ujjayini.

You were born in Ujjayini. . . .

As a Boy . . .

As a Girl . . .

You and your parents and siblings live with your father's parents and his brothers and their families. The extended family may have one large house or a group of houses. There may be many servants. Everyone treats you with kindness and affection.

Between the ages of eight and twelve you are initiated, then you begin your formal education. You may go to live at your teacher's home or at a monastery. Your main studies are religious. Or you may stay home and learn your father's trade or become an apprentice.

▼

In your early twenties, your studies are finished. You return home and begin life as an adult. As soon as possible, you marry a girl chosen for you by your parents. You earn a living according to the traditions of your family and class. You take part in regular religious rituals with the other men of your family. You spend a great deal of time socializing. When your father dies, you become head of your own household.

▼

Once your sons have sons, you are expected to devote yourself to religion. You may leave your home and live in the forest as a hermit, and when you are very old you may become a wandering ascetic. Or you may choose to remain at home and simply live a less active life.

You remain at home and learn the art of homemaking and certain cultural accomplishments. You probably also learn to read and write. Between the ages of puberty and sixteen you marry a man chosen for you by your parents. You go to live with your husband's family.

▼

You become pregnant as soon as possible. You devote yourself to caring for your husband and children. You may have to share your husband with one or more other wives, but all of you help one another with child care and housework. You rarely leave the house without your husband.

▼

If your husband dies before you, you are not allowed to marry again. You remain with your husband's family, but you cannot attend festivals, wear jewelry or bright-colored clothing, or eat more than one simple meal a day. You are avoided by everyone except your children.

When you die, your body is considered impure. It is carried away and cremated by untouchables. Mourners circle the funeral pyre counterclockwise as scriptures are read. Three days after the cremation, the charred bones and ashes are thrown into a river.

At the same time, a husband was expected to care well for his wife (or wives), to love and cherish her, to give her whatever fine clothes and jewelry he could afford, and to be as gentle as possible with her. It was said that the gods would not accept the sacrifice of a man who beat his wife. Moreover, wives were frequently honored as the source of all joys and of all that would help men in this world and the next.

Even so, women had few rights. According to the laws, they were never independent. An unmarried girl was under the authority of her father; a wife was under the authority of her husband; a widow was under the authority of her sons. A woman was allowed to own little more than her clothes and jewelry and usually could inherit nothing but her mother's clothes and jewelry. If she drank, played games, or left the house without her husband's permission, she could be fined. If she spoke to a man other than her husband, in some situations she could be flogged.

Woeful Widows

The worst thing that could happen to a woman, though, was for her husband to die. A widow was forbidden to remarry; it was believed that if she did, she would endanger her dead husband's soul. In addition, it was hoped that she and her husband would marry each other again in the next life, so she was expected to remain faithful to him.

In the meantime the widow lived a miserable life. According to the sacred law, she was supposed to sleep on the ground and eat only one plain meal a day. She was supposed to spend all her time praying and performing rituals for her husband's soul. Her husband's family, with whom she still lived, watched over her constantly to make sure she kept up these ascetic habits. If she did not, both she and her husband would suffer unhappy rebirths. To make matters worse, a widow was believed to bring bad luck to everyone except her children. At least partly because of the miseries of widowhood, it became increasingly common from Gupta times onward for Indian widows to burn themselves to death on their husbands' funeral pyres.

CHAPTER FIVE

A LASTING INFLUENCE

This splendid temple was founded around 200 C.E. on the site where the Buddha attained enlightenment. It was rebuilt during the Gupta period and restored many times over the following centuries.

Although the Gupta Empire had disappeared by 550, it left a great cultural legacy. Gupta architecture laid the foundation for later developments in temple design and construction. Gupta sculpture and painting were imitated throughout the Middle Ages and, to some extent, even up to the present. Kalidasa is still acknowledged as India's greatest poet and dramatist. These are only a few of the lasting contributions that the Guptas made to the culture of India—and the world.

Passing on the Traditions

As the Gupta age saw the creation of important new works of literature, it also saw the preservation and refinement of older works. In this period India's two great epics, the *Mahabharata* (muh-HAH-bah-ruh-tuh) and the *Ramayana* (RAH-mah-yuh-nuh), received their final form. These poems had been preserved in oral tradition for hundreds of years. Their Gupta editors ensured that they would continue to entertain and inspire Indians—and others—for hundreds more. They are now classics of world literature. In the United States and Europe as well as in Asia, films, audio recordings, and dances have been made of both epics in recent years.

At about 100,000 stanzas, the *Mahabharata* is the longest poem in world literature. It is India's national epic. Its main plot involves the struggle of the five Pandava brothers to gain and hold the throne of the Kuru kingdom (the region around modern Delhi).

In this scene from the Ramayana, *painted in the seventeenth century, Rama and his monkey allies fight against an army of demons.*

The *Mahabharata* also contains many independent episodes. The most famous of these is the *Bhagavad Gita* (BAG-uh-vad GEE-tah). This is a sermon given by the god Krishna to encourage one of the Pandava brothers, Arjuna, before a great battle. It deals with the nature of dharma and is still today one of the most important texts of Hinduism. Other episodes tell stories of deities and of legendary kings and queens.

The *Ramayana,* which every modern Indian schoolchild knows, is a quarter of the length of the *Mahabharata.* It tells the story of Rama, an incarnation of the god Vishnu, and his wife Sita. Rama, heir of the kingdom of Kosala, wins the hand of Sita in a great archery contest. They live happily until Rama's father is forced to banish and disinherit him, then become hermits in a forest. During this time Rama destroys many demons. Their king, Ravana, decides to take vengeance and kidnaps Sita. Rama, aided by monkeys, searches everywhere for his wife. At last the general of the monkeys, Hanuman, finds her. Rama and an army of monkeys fight a fierce battle with Ravana, killing him and rescuing Sita.

Unfortunately, Sita has been living under the roof of a man other than her husband. Even though she has remained faithful to Rama, the sacred law demands that he turn her away. She throws

THE UNIVERSITY OF NALANDA

Nalanda had long been one of the sacred sites of Buddhism, since the Buddha had visited it several times during his life. But it seems that Kumara Gupta helped found the first great monastery there. Other Gupta rulers added to it, donating dormitories for students.

By the seventh century, Nalanda was a complex of six monasteries and was the greatest university in all of Asia. Its educational facilities included lecture halls, three libraries, and an observatory. Courses were available not only in Buddhist teachings and philosophy but also in Hindu philosophy, logic, grammar, literature, architecture, art, medicine, mathematics, astronomy, and agriculture. The entrance exams were extremely difficult, and only 20 to 30 percent of the applicants were admitted. Poor students were given free tuition, room and board, medicine, and clothes.

Until it was destroyed by Muslim invaders in the twelfth century, the University of herself onto a funeral pyre, but the fire god, Agni, refuses to burn her. With this divine proof of her innocence, she can finally be reunited with Rama. They return home, and Rama peacefully takes his place as king.

Although Rama is completely convinced of Sita's faithfulness to him, his people are not. As king, it is his first duty to please the people, and so, with great regret, he banishes Sita. She goes to a hermitage, where she gives birth to two boys. Rama eventually finds her and acknowledges their sons. Sita then calls upon the Earth, her mother, to swallow her up. Soon afterward Rama returns to heaven, resuming the form of Vishnu.

Both of the epics were made up of many stories from many sources. More old tales were brought together in the sacred books

Ruins are all that is left of the once-magnificent University of Nalanda.

Nalanda remained the most important educational center of Asia. From Nalanda, Indian culture spread throughout Asia, for students came from as far away as China, Japan, and Korea to study there. It is largely thanks to this university founded by the Guptas that Buddhism is today a world religion.

This eighteenth-century painting illustrates a story from the Puranas. *Shiva, wearing animal skins and his necklace of skulls, has markings on his forehead similar to those still worn by many of his worshipers.*

known as the *Puranas* (pu-RAH-nuhs), meaning "Ancient Stories." Eventually there were eighteen *Puranas,* and the earliest were given form during the Gupta age.

The *Puranas* contain a mixture of poetry, philosophy, religious instruction, folklore, imagination, myth, and legend. They were the first Hindu scriptures that were available to everyone, including women and the lower classes. The *Puranas* became the basis of popular Hindu mythology as it exists even to this day.

Another collection of stories was the *Panchatantra* (PAN-chuh-TAN-truh). This work contains more than eighty fables, in which most of the characters are animals that talk and act like people. Aside from being highly entertaining, the tales also demonstrate *niti* (NEE-tih), "the art of intelligent living."

No one knows exactly when the *Panchatantra* was written, but it was undoubtedly very popular in Gupta India. From there its popularity spread to the Persian and Arab worlds and to Mediterranean Europe. In 1570 it became the first work of Indian literature published in English. In every country where the *Panchatantra* was translated, it had a great influence on the writers and storytellers there. Back in India, in the Middle Ages it was used as a textbook for learning Sanskrit.

Advancing the Sciences

Some of the Gupta period's most far-reaching and lasting achievements were in the sciences. In the fourth century, Sushruta composed a basic medical textbook. Traditional Indian medicine, called *ayurveda* (EYE-yer-VEE-duh) and still practiced today, is essentially the same as Sushruta's system.

Indian doctors of Gupta times had a very high level of medical knowledge. They had access to many drugs from animal, mineral, and plant sources. They encouraged cleanliness and knew that fresh air and light were necessary for good health. They understood the importance of the spinal cord and, to some extent, the workings of the nervous system. They were experts at setting bones and repairing lost or injured noses, lips, and ears. This knowledge was passed down to doctors of later times. By the eighteenth century, Indian doctors were teaching Europeans the art of plastic surgery.

Gupta observatories probably resembled this one in Jaipur, which was constructed in the eighteenth century.

In astronomy, too, great strides were made. By Gupta times India had adopted the Greco-Roman zodiac. From this period on, Indians were extremely interested in astrology and its uses in making predictions, choosing the best times for special events, and the like. Because of this, the stars and planets were more closely observed than ever before, and soon astrology and Indian mathematics combined to yield new discoveries. In the fifth century the great astronomer and mathematician Aryabhata (AR-yuh-buh-tuh) stated that the earth was round, that it rotated on its axis, and that it revolved around the sun. It would be centuries before European astronomers would reach the same conclusions.

It is in the field of mathematics that Gupta culture has made the biggest practical impact on the world. An anonymous fourth-century mathematician and Aryabhata both wrote mathematics books that described a simple numerical system with a zero and nine digits. These are the so-called Arabic numerals that are used all over the world today. The Arabs, in fact, called mathematics "the Indian science"; they learned the numerals from India and then passed them on to Europe.

The concept of zero and the new number symbols allowed another important innovation: place notation for the tens, hundreds, thousands, and so on. This made it possible to perform all sorts of mathematical operations that could not be done before. For example, try to imagine doing long division with Roman numerals, which have no place notation.

In India the study and use of numbers evolved further than in any other ancient culture except perhaps those of the Maya and the Babylonians, who also discovered zero. Gupta mathematicians developed algebra and trigonometry. They also worked with negative and abstract numbers.

Indian mathematics changed the use of numbers throughout the world. The decimal system pioneered in Gupta times was the foundation of all later mathematical developments. These, in turn, made possible many of the scientific discoveries and inventions that we take for granted today.

Preserving the Culture

One constant throughout most of Indian history has been village life. In both ancient and modern times, the majority of India's people have lived in rural villages. The Hunas invaded, the Gupta Empire fell apart, small kings warred against one another, and eventually Muslim conquerors took over. Out in the countryside, though, the people followed the old ways, helping to sustain the Indian cultural identity—right up to the present.

In the Gupta period, a typical village was made up of a group of huts clustered around a well or pond. Nearby was an open area with some trees. The entire village was surrounded by a wall or stockade. The wall was there to keep out elephants, tigers, and, in western India, lions. In some parts of the country the wall was also a defense against the raids of wild tribes from the forests and hills.

Life in India's rural villages has continued with little change since Gupta times.

Most of the villagers were peasants who worked their own small family farms. Outside the village wall spread their fields. Here they raised wheat, barley, rice, or millet as staple food crops. Cotton was the staple textile crop. Lentils, peas, beans, leafy vegetables, gourds, and sugarcane were also grown. Mango orchards were common. In the pastures beyond the fields, cattle grazed. They were used to pull plows and carts and to provide dairy products, which were a very important part of the diet.

A village was a close-knit community with a strong group spirit. It had its own guardian deity, usually a goddess. Its social center was the village temple. A headman and probably a small council governed the village. They were completely independent of the king and his provincial governors. In fact, so long as villagers paid their taxes, they seem to have been mostly left alone by the central government. These were some of the characteristics of village life that allowed it to continue to the present with little change, no matter who was ruling India.

After the Gupta Empire decayed, there was no long-lasting unification of northern India until the Muslim conquests of the twelfth century. When foreign rulers and foreign ways had charge

THE LAST GLIMMER OF THE GOLDEN AGE

Although the Gupta Empire had ceased to exist by 550, in the next century its glory was briefly revived by Harsha Vardhana. Harsha was the son of a local chief who fought against the Hunas as well as against other area chiefs. In 606, at the age of sixteen, Harsha succeeded his father. Over the next six years he conquered most of what had been the Gupta Empire.

Harsha was a benevolent ruler in the tradition of Chandra Gupta II. During his reign northern India again enjoyed prosperity, light taxation, and public services such as hospitals and roadside rest houses. In dealing with crime, Harsha believed in both justice and mercy. Even when five hundred Brahmans were arrested for plotting against him, he pardoned all but the ringleaders. And like the great Gupta emperor, Harsha was a devoted patron of the arts and sciences. He himself wrote Sanskrit dramas, three of which have survived to the present. Harsha was a devout Buddhist, but he also worshiped the Hindu gods Shiva and Surya. He was tolerant of all religions and held a gathering where representatives of India's various religious groups met to discuss their beliefs.

In 647 Harsha was murdered. He had no lawful heir, so his realm quickly came under attack and disintegrated. Northern India once more became a land of warring chieftains, not to be united again under native rule until the twentieth century.

of the land, Indians became even more deeply attached to their own ways. Caste rules became very strict, and remained so until the twentieth century. Being a member of a caste, like being a member of a family, helped an Indian maintain a sense of identity. The devout Hinduism that flowered under the Guptas became even stronger. Krishna and Rama, the most heroic of the gods, were worshiped more than ever. And since the rituals of Hinduism were performed mainly by individuals and families and did not depend on a large national organization, the religion was

The timelessness of Hinduism is seen in this ritual of devotion that has a statue of a cow, the most sacred of all animals, as its focus.

A shraddha *ritual, nearly the same today as it was fifteen hundred and more years ago. The rice balls, called pinda, are laid on leaves. The sacred thread can be clearly seen on the two men at the left.*

able to survive Muslim supremacy. As a result, Hinduism continues to flourish in modern India and has many followers in other parts of the world as well.

Today, much has changed since Gupta times. India is now an independent, democratic nation. Caste has been outlawed. Women have equal rights. But the best aspects of the ancient culture live on, and the glories of India's golden age continue to be a source of national pride and inspiration.

The Guptas: A Chronology

320 C.E.   The Gupta Era begins; Chandra Gupta rules

335–376   Reign of Samudra Gupta

376   Shakas defeat Rama Gupta; Chandra Gupta II comes to the throne

388   Chandra Gupta II defeats the Shakas

401–410   Fa-hsien travels through India

415   Kumara Gupta's reign begins

453   First Huna invasion

455–467   Reign of Skanda Gupta

467   Pura Gupta rules for less than a year

467–473   Narasimha Gupta's reign

473–476   Kumara Gupta II's reign

476–495   Budha Gupta's reign

495   Second Huna invasion

500–533   Hunas in control of western half of northern India; Gupta power limited to a small area in the east

533   Yashodharman defeats the Hunas once and for all, takes over most of the Gupta Empire

550   Gupta kings rule locally, but the empire is gone

NOTE: Sources vary considerably for dates from this period. Dates given are approximate.

GLOSSARY

apsaras (AP-suh-ruhs): a beautiful, divine young woman of the heavens. *Apsarases* sometimes came to earth to marry human men.

ascetic (uh-SEH-tihk): a person who chooses to live in poverty and devote himself or herself to religion. Ascetics often put themselves through many penances, or hardships, as a way to purify themselves.

ayurveda (EYE-yer-VEE-duh): traditional Indian medicine

bodhisattva (BOD-hih-SAT-vuh): a being who has attained enlightenment but instead of permanently entering Nirvana decides to remain in a state where he or she can help others toward enlightenment

Brahman (BRAH-muhn): a member of the priestly class

chandalas (chan-DAH-luhs): a group of "untouchables," not included in the class system, who cremated corpses

Deccan (DEH-kuhn): the central portion of India. (Sometimes southern India is also referred to as part of the Deccan; otherwise it is called the Peninsula.)

dharma (DAR-muh): righteousness, justice, truth, the order of things, sacred law, ethical behavior, sacred duty

ghee: butter that has been melted and then strained to remove milk solids and butter fat. Unlike regular butter, ghee can keep indefinitely without refrigeration.

guru (GUR-oo): a learned Brahman teacher

incarnate (in-KAR-nayt): to take on flesh and live on earth as a human or animal

inscription (in-SKRIHP-shuhn): words carved on a monument or building

karma (KAR-muh): the effect that a person's past actions, either in this life or in a previous one, have on his or her present and future

Kshatriya (KSHUH-trih-yuh): a member of the warrior class

mudra (MU-drah): a symbolic hand gesture

Nirvana (ner-VAH-nuh): the ideal state of perfect knowledge, understanding, and oneness with the universe; enlightenment

puja (POO-jah): a ritual of worship and service to an image of a deity

purgatory (PUR-guh-tor-ee): an in-between state after death where souls are purified through suffering

reincarnation (REE-in-kar-NAY-shuhn): rebirth of the soul into a new body after death

relief: a form of sculpture in which the images project out from a flat surface

shakti (SHAHK-tee): a god's vital energy, the source of his power, embodied by the goddess to whom he is married

shraddha (SHRAHD-huh): a monthly ritual in which a householder honors his ancestors

Shudra (SHOO-druh): a member of the lowest class

Tara: savioress; the wife of bodhisattva Avalokiteshvara

Vaishya (VYSH-yuh): a member of the merchant and farming class

Vedas (VEE-duhs): collections of religious hymns and related material, composed between 1500 and 900 B.C.E. The oldest and most sacred Veda is the *Rig Veda*.

yaksha (YAK-shuh): a semidivine earth spirit, somewhat like a gnome or fairy

FOR FURTHER READING

Bond, Ruskin. *Tales and Legends from India.* New York: Franklin Watts, 1982.

Galbraith, Catherine Atwater, and Rama Mehta. *India Now and through Time.* Boston: Houghton Mifflin, 1980.

Haviland, Virginia. *Favorite Fairy Tales Told in India.* Boston: Little, Brown, 1973.

*Lal, P., trans. *Great Sanskrit Plays in Modern Translation.* New York: New Directions, 1964.

Reed, Gwendolyn. *The Talkative Beasts: Myths, Fables, and Poems of India.* New York: Lothrop, Lee & Shepard, 1969.

*Ryder, Arthur W., trans. *The Panchatantra.* Chicago: University of Chicago Press, 1925.

Sarin, Amita Vohra. *India: An Ancient Land, a New Nation.* Minneapolis: Dillon Press, 1984.

*Schulberg, Lucille. *Historic India.* New York: Time-Life Books, 1968.

Shepard, Aaron. *Savitri: A Tale of Ancient India.* Morton Grove, Illinois: Albert Whitman, 1992.

Snelling, John. *Buddhism.* New York: Bookwright Press, 1986.

Upadhyay, Asha. *Tales from India.* New York: Random House, 1971.

*Although these books were written for adults, they contain much to interest younger readers as well.

BIBLIOGRAPHY

Basham, A. L. *The Wonder That Was India.* Third revised edition. New York: Taplinger Publishing Company, 1967.

Bhattacharya, Sachchidananda. *A Dictionary of Indian History.* New York: George Braziller, 1967.

de Bary, Wm. Theodore, ed. *Sources of Indian Tradition.* Vol. 1. New York: Columbia University Press, 1958.

Goetz, Hermann. "Gupta, School of," in *Encyclopedia of World Art.* New York, Toronto, London: McGraw-Hill, 1963.

Hawkridge, Emma. *Indian Gods and Kings.* 1935; reprint. Freeport, New York: Books for Libraries Press, 1968.

Lal, P., trans. *Great Sanskrit Plays in Modern Translation.* New York: New Directions, 1964.

Parrinder, Geoffrey, ed. *World Religions: From Ancient History to the Present.* New York: Facts on File Publications, 1971.

Ryder, Arthur W., trans. *The Panchatantra.* Chicago: University of Chicago Press, 1925.

Schulberg, Lucille. *Historic India.* New York: Time-Life Books, 1968.

Sen, Gertrude Emerson. *The Pageant of India's History.* New York: David McKay, 1948.

Smith, Bardwell L., ed. *Essays on Gupta Culture.* Delhi: Motilal Banarsidass, 1983.

Watson, Francis. *A Concise History of India.* New York: Charles Scribner's Sons, 1975.

INDEX

Page numbers for illustrations are in boldface

ABOUT THE AUTHOR

Kathryn Hinds has always been fascinated by ancient cultures. As a child she dreamed of becoming an archaeologist or a writer. She grew up near Rochester, New York, then moved to New York City to study music and writing at Barnard College. She did graduate work in comparative literature at the City University of New York. For several years she has worked as a freelance editor of children's books. She also writes poetry, which has been published in a number of magazines. Ms. Hinds now lives in north Georgia with her husband, their son, and two cats.